# I THINK MICE ARE RATI
## An anthology of poetry



Mice *are* rather nice. When you think about it. For [illegible] around the world have felt this way and a wealth of poetry has been written celebrating, both in town and country, the humble, little mouse with its silky ears and round, beady eyes.

*I Think Mice Are Rather Nice* contains poems by Laurie Lee, Philip Larkin, John Betjeman, Edith Sitwell, e e cummings, Robert Burns, Eleanor Farjeon, Christina Rossetti, John Clare, Geoffrey Chaucer, Leonard Clark, Ian Serraillier, Albert Rowe, Clifford Dyment, Gregory Harrison and many others. In addition to selecting the poetry Robert Field has illustrated this fascinating anthology with numerous delightful line drawings. Together, poetry and illustrations should convince the reader that mice really *are* rather nice. When you think about it.

Robert Field was born at Hayes, in Kent, in 1939. After a number of years working for a firm of music publishers in London he enrolled as a mature student to train as a teacher. He is now deputy head of a Surrey school and in addition to his work with children has given numerous courses on art and craft for teachers. In 1988 after many years of studying Roman history he wrote and illustrated his first book, *Geometric Patterns From Roman Mosaics,* published by Tarquin Publications, which rapidly became a popular success. He has illustrated two other Triple Cat books, *Clap Hands for the Singing Molecatcher* and *Strathalder : A Highland Estate,* both by Roderick Grant.

# I THINK MICE ARE RATHER NICE

## An anthology of poetry

Selected and illustrated by

## Robert Field

I think mice
Are rather nice.
Their tails are long,
Their faces small
They haven't any
Chins at all.
Their ears are pink,
Their teeth are white,
They run about
The house at night.
They nibble things
They shouldn't touch
And no one seems
To like them much

But I think mice
Are nice.

***Rose Fyleman***

TRIPLE CAT PUBLISHING

First published by Triple Cat Publishing, 1990



Designed by Robert Field

Typeset in Optima by Saxon Printing Ltd., Heritage Gate, Derby

Printed and bound by Biddles Ltd., Guildford and King's Lynn

**British Library Cataloguing in Publication Data**

I think mice are rather nice: an anthology of poetry.
1. Poetry in English. Special subjects. Mice – Anthologies
I. Field, Robert 1939-
821.008036

ISBN 1-871936-04-7

**Triple Cat Publishing,**
**3 Back Lane Cottages,**
**Bucks Horn Oak,**
**Farnham,**
**Surrey, GU10 4LN.**

# INTRODUCTION

Mice are rather nice. When you stop to think about it. Even the much-maligned house mouse has a personality all of its own in its furry, scurrying body. True, they get into awkward places and do all manner of irritating things. The trouble is – they never stop to think. Just tear at the wrapper on the sugar bag, nibble the biscuits, rip the side from a packet of lentils, run away with the newly-sown garden peas. As a result the wrath of God descends on them; at least, the wrath of humans because, presumably, God views their mischief with the same benign eye he casts on the equally unpredictable behaviour of many other creatures – two and four legged – on this earth. In the house, in the garden, in the woods and fields, along the hedgerows, down by the sides of roads, the mouse family – house mouse, field mouse, harvest mouse and dormouse – live their frenetic, fearful lives; wary of man, in terror of slinking cat and chattering weasel. Theirs is no easy life. The odds are decidedly stacked against them.

But whatever certain individuals may feel about mice (and it's true there are some who regard them with feelings ranging from loathing to dread) there is no doubt about it; the humble little mouse with silky ears and round,beady eyes, has been a favourite with many people – child and adult – down the span of centuries. A delight to see – shy, hesitant peeping eyes staring from skirting board or the depths of a leafy bank; a pleasure to read about – to laugh at and cry over – in prose and poetry.

This selection of poems reflects the world of the mouse as seen by poets of various generations. For those with a special affinity for Robert Burns' "wee, sleekit, cowrin', tim'rous beastie" this book is offered as a reward for your faith. You will need no enlightenment. For those who shrink from the sound of scurrying feet beneath the floorboards or high above in the loft and think murderous thoughts when the larder is raided at dead of night by shadowy, squeaking figures perhaps, well just perhaps, you may be converted, or at least think again.

Because mice really *are* rather nice. When you think about it. Honestly.

***Robert Field***

# ACKNOWLEDGMENTS

The publishers and I would like to thank all those who have given permission for their poems to appear in this anthology. We have made every effort to trace the copyright holders for permission to use their work. We would be most grateful to learn of any instances where an incomplete or incorrect acknowledgment has been made. We would like to thank the following for permission to include poems in their copyright:

Steuart Allin for *Brother Mouse.*
Macmillan & Co for *The Prayer of the Mouse* from PRAYERS FROM THE ARK by Carmen Berners de Gasztold translated by Rumer Godden.
John Murray (Publishers) Ltd for *Diary of a Church Mouse* from COLLECTED POEMS by John Betjeman.
Dobson Books Ltd for *In Autumn* from GOOD COMPANY by Leonard Clark.
*The Mouse* by Elizabeth Coatsworth reprinted by permission of Coward-McCann from COMPASS ROSE by Elizabeth Coatsworth, copyright 1929 by Coward-McCann, Inc., © renewed 1957 by Elizabeth Coatsworth.
*The Satin Mice Creaking Last Summer's Grass* reprinted with permission of Macmillan Publishing Company from ON THE GREEN CARPET by Robert P. Tristram Coffin.
William Collins Sons & Co. Ltd for *The Dormouse* and *Three Mice* by Charlotte Druitt Cole.
Elizabeth Critchfield for *Mouse, Nunc Dimmitis,* and *Thoughts of a Well-Read Cat.*
Grafton Books, a division of the Collins Publishing Group for *Me up at does* from COMPLETE POEMS VOL II (1936-62) by e e cummings.
J.M.Dent & Sons for *Mouse* from POEMS 1935-48 by Clifford Dyment.
David Higham Associates Limited for *Invitation to a Mouse* from INVITATION TO A MOUSE AND OTHER POEMS by Eleanor Farjeon.
The Society of Authors as the literary representatives of the Estate of Rose Fyleman for *Mice* from 51 NEW NURSERY RHYMES published by Methuen.
Gregory Harrison for *The Mice* from POSTING LETTERS published by Oxford University Press.
*The Dormouse* by S.Holroyd taken from POEMS FOR MOVEMENT, edited by E.J.M. Woodland, reproduced by kind permission of Unwin Hyman Ltd.
Iain Kendell for *Small Preference.*

Faber & Faber Ltd for *Take One Home for the Kiddies* from THE WHITSUN WEDDINGS by Philip Larkin.
Andre Deutsch Ltd for *Day of these Days* from SELECTED POEMS (1983) by Laurie Lee.
*Mouse* from SELECTED POEMS by Kenneth MacKenzie by kind permission of the publishers Angus and Robertson (UK).
Acknowledgments are due to Leslie Norris for *Mice in the Hay* taken from his book NORRIS'S ARK.
Richard Rieu for *The Lament of the White Mouse* by E.V.Rieu from THE PUFFIN QUARTET OF POETS.
*The Meadow Mouse* by Theodore Roethke reprinted by permission of Faber & Faber Ltd from THE COLLECTED POEMS OF THEODORE ROETHKE.
Albert Rowe for *The Fieldmouse.*
David Higham Associates Limited and Clive Sansom for *Harvest Mouse* from AN ENGLISH YEAR published by Chatto and Windus and *Mice and Cat* from THE GOLDEN UNICORN published by Methuen.
Ian Serraillier for *Death of the Cat* from THE MONSTER HORSE published by Oxford University Press.
*Madam Mouse Trots* by Edith Sitwell is reprinted by permission of Duckworth & Co. Ltd.

# IN AUTUMN

Over wayside hedges trail now
old man's beard, spiders' webs;
staring berries of nightshade, thorn,
hang in frail sunlight, redder than
twitching snout of harvest mouse
gleaning stray corn stalks,
or coral lip of toadstool, splashed leaf;
copper chrysanthemums burnish the chill air.
A man is picking apples, one by one,
in the crisp orchard behind the house,
laying them to bed in mealy loft
where hives smell of smoke and honeycomb,
and overhead the great, invincible V
of geese flying with snow from the sea.

***Leonard Clark***

# THE HARVEST MOUSE

A sleek, brown acrobat, he climbs
The golden cornstalk till it sways
And sags beneath him. As it swings,
His tail-end twines a neighbour stalk
And balancing with tail and claw
He climbs aloft until he finds
The crisp, ripe, bristly ear of corn;
Then lies along its tilting length,
As if all corn-ears were created
For mice to nibble at ... and nibbles.

***Clive Sansom***

# THE WOOD MOUSE

Do ye know the little Wood-Mouse,
    That pretty little thing,
That sits among the forest leaves
    Beside the forest spring? ...

'Tis a timid, gentle creature,
    And seldom comes in sight;
It has a long and wiry tail,
    And eyes both black and bright.

It makes its nest of soft, dry moss
    In a hole both deep and strong;
And there it sits secure and warm
    The dreary winter long ...

In the Hedge-Sparrow's nest he sits
    When the summer brood has fled,
And picks the berries from the bough
    Of the hawthorn over-head.

I saw a little Wood-Mouse once
    Like Oberon in his hall,
With the green, green moss beneath his feet
    Sit under a mushroom tall ...

I saw that He regardeth them –
    Those creatures weak and small,
Their table in the wild is spread
    By Him who cares for all.

***Mary Howitt***

# MOUSE'S NEST

I found a ball of grass among the hay
And progged it as I passed and went away;
And when I looked I fancied something stirred,
And turned again and hoped to catch the bird –
When out an old mouse bolted in the wheats
With all her young ones hanging at her teats;
She looked so odd and so grotesque to me,
I ran and wondered what the thing could be,
And pushed the knapweed bunches where I stood.
Then the mouse hurried from the craking brood,
The young ones squeaked, and as I went away,
She found her nest again among the hay.
The water o'er the pebbles scarce could run
And broad old cesspools glittered in the sun.

***John Clare***

# THE FIELDMOUSE

When the moon shines oe'r the corn
And the beetle drones his horn,
And the flittermice swift fly,
And the nightjars swooping cry,
And the young hares run and leap,
We waken from our sleep.

And we climb with tiny feet
And we munch the green corn sweet
With startled eyes for fear
The white owl should fly near,
Or long slim weasel spring
Upon us where we swing.

We do not hurt at all;
Is there not room for all
Within the happy world?
All day we lie close curled
In drowsy sleep, nor rise
Till through the dusky skies
The moon shines oe'r the corn
And the beetle drones his horn.

***William Sharp***

# THE FIELDMOUSE

Where the acorn tumbles down,
Where the ash tree sheds its berry,
With your fur so soft and brown,
With your eye so round and merry,
Scarcely moving the long grass,
Fieldmouse, I can see you pass.

Little thing, in what dark den,
Lie you all the winter sleeping?
Till warm weather comes again,
Then once more I see you peeping
Round about the tall tree roots,
Nibbling at their fallen fruits.

Fieldmouse, fieldmouse, do not go,
Where the farmer stacks his treasure,
Find the nut that falls below,
Eat the acorn at your pleasure,
But you must not steal the grain
He has stacked with so much pain.

Make your hole where mosses spring,
Underneath the tall oak's shadow,
Pretty, quiet, harmless thing,
Play about the sunny meadow.
Keep away from corn and house,
None will harm you, little mouse.

***Cecil Frances Alexander***

# SUMMER EVENING

The frog, half fearful, jumps across the path,
And little mouse that leaves its hole at eve
Nimbles with timid dread beneath the swath;
My rustling steps awhile their joys deceive,
Till past – and then the cricket sings more strong,
And grasshoppers in merry moods still wear
The short night weary with their fretting song.
Up from behind the mole-hill jumps the hare,
Cheat of his chosen bed, and from the bank
The yellowhammer flutters in short fears
From off its nest hid in the grasses rank,
And drops again when no more noise it hears.
Thus nature's human link and endless thrall,
Proud man, still seems the enemy of all.

***John Clare***

# FIELDMOUSE

I am too enormous for the gleaming
blackness of your eyes to take in. Unaware
you trickle up to me searching
for food.
          I lift my foot, and at once
you drift under it, safe in the cool
roofed dark.
          You edge out. I put down a crumb
close to your etched front paws. Quickly
you hug it and, hunched up, begin
to eat at starving speed, fur grey
and fine as ashes, shoulders bright
as acorn.
          You devour the crumb, then roll
satisfied, thistledown in a gentle breeze,
slowly back to the haven of the hedge.

I'm glad you're as unaware of the hawk
that hunts you by day, unaware of the taloned
owl that hunts you by night, as you are
of me, that you live in such serene
innocence between a death and a death.

***Albert Rowe***

# TO A MOUSE
## On turning her up in her nest with the plough, November 1785

Wee, sleekit, cow'rin', tim'rous beastie,
O what a panic's in thy breastie!
Thou need na start awa sae hasty,
    Wi' bickering brattle!
I wad be laith to rin an' chase thee
    Wi' murd'ring pattle!

I'm truly sorry Man's dominion
Has broken Nature's social union,
An' justifies that ill opinion,
    Which makes thee startle,
At me, thy poor, earth-born companion,
    An' fellow-mortal!

I doubt na, whiles, but thou may thieve;
What then? poor beastie, thou maun live!
A daimen-icker in a thrave
    'S a sma' request:
I'll get a blessin' wi' the lave,
    And never miss't!

Thy wee-bit housie, too, in ruin!
Its silly wa's the win's are strewin'!
An' naething, now, to big a new ane,
O' foggage green!
An' bleak December's winds ensuin',
Baith snell an' keen!

Thou saw the fields laid bare and waste,
An' weary winter comin' fast,
An' cozie here, beneath the blast,
Thou thought to dwell,
Till crash! the cruel coulter past
Out thro' thy cell.

That wee-bit heap o' leaves and stibble
Has cost thee mony a weary nibble!
Now thou's turned out, for a' thy trouble,
But house or hald,
To thole the Winter's sleety dribble,
an' cranreuch cauld!

But, Mousie, thou are no thy lane,
In proving foresight may be vain:
The best laid schemes o' Mice an' Men
Gang aft a-gley,
An' lea'e us nought but grief an' pain
For promised joy.

Still thou art blest compared wi' me!
The present only toucheth thee:
But Och! I backward cast my e'e
On prospects drear!
An' forward tho' I canna see,
I guess an' fear!

***Robert Burns***

# EPITAPH ON A DORMOUSE
## Which some children were to bury

In paper case,
Hard by this place,
Dead a poor dormouse lies;
And soon or late,
Summoned by fate,
Each prince, each monarch dies.

Ye sons of verse,
While I rehearse,
Attend instructive rhyme;
No sins had Dor
To answer for,
Repent of yours in time.

***Anon 1765***

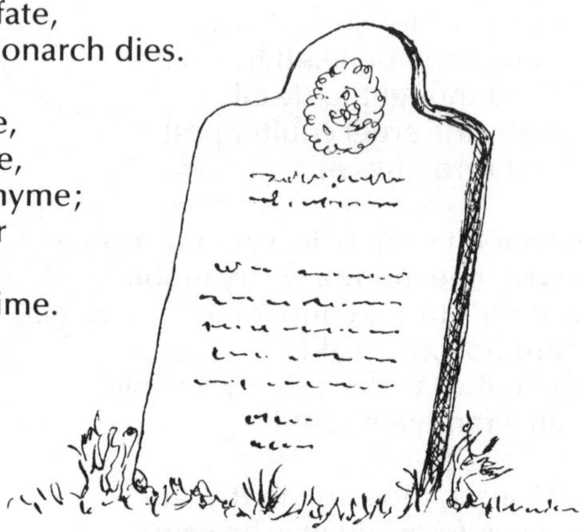

The North wind doth blow,
And we shall have snow,
And what will the dormouse do then,
poor thing?
Rolled up in a ball,
In his nest snug and small.
He'll sleep till the winter is past,
poor thing.

***Anon***

# THE DORMOUSE

The Dormouse felt so sleepy
    Nid-nodding went his head,
He said "Good night" to everyone,
    And cuddled up in bed.

Down fell the icy raindrops,
    The cold wind whistled round;
The Dormouse in his snuggly bed,
    Lay sleeping safe and sound.

There he was found one morning
    By Jeremy and Jane;
They whispered low, then on tip-toe,
    They crept away again.

They filled a bag with acorns,
    And hid it in the brakes,
So that the little Dormouse,
    May find it when he wakes.

***Charlotte Druitt Cole***

# THE DORMOUSE

All winter through the dormouse sleeps
Curled up in his hole so warm and deep.
He raises his head and sniffs the air
To see if his friends are safe elsewhere.

No sign of danger, so now uncurled
He creeps outside to view the world.
The flowers are out, he gleefully sees,
And tiny buds have burst on the trees.

Shyly he strolls about the wood
His nose to the ground, oh it smells so good!
He looks up at the sky so blue and white
And down at the ground so green and bright.

When he's eaten his store of acorns and nuts
It's back to his hole over hillocks and ruts,
Then he curls up small and closes his eyes,
In his nest so cosy he quietly lies.

***S. Holroyd***

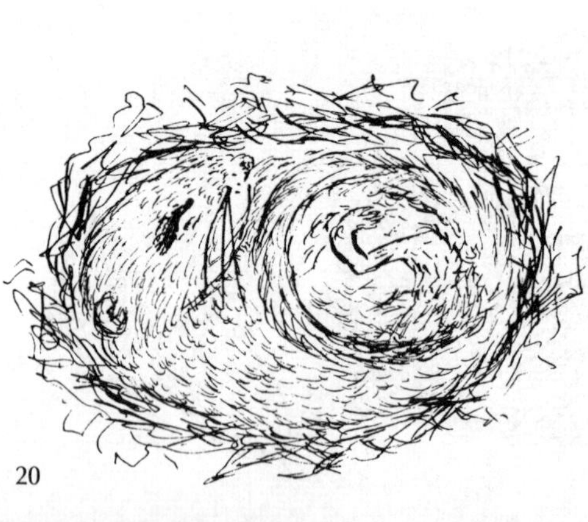

# THE DORMOUSE

The little Dormouse is tawny red;
He makes against winter a nice snug bed,
He makes his bed in a mossy bank
Where the plants in summer grow tall and rank;
Away from the light, far underground,
His sleep through winter is quiet and sound;
And when all above him freezes and snows,
What is it to him? For he nought of it knows.
And till the cold time of the winter is gone,
The little Dormouse keeps sleeping on.
But at last, in the fresh breezy days of the Spring,
When the green leaves bud and the merry birds sing,
And the dread of the winter is over and past,
The little Dormouse peeps out at last:
Out of his snug quiet burrow he wends,
And looks all about for neighbours and friends;
Then he says, as he sits at the foot of a larch,
"'Tis a beautiful day for the first day in March!
The violet is blowing, the blue sky is clear,
The lark is up-springing, his carol I hear;
And in the fields are the lamb and the foal;
I'm glad I'm not sleeping down in my hole!"
Then away he runs, in his merry mood,
Over the fields and into the wood,
To find any grain there may chance to be,
Or any small berry that hangs on the tree ...
So, from early morning till late at night,
Has the poor little creature its own delight.
Looking down to the earth and up to the sky,
Thinking, "Ah! what a happy Dormouse am I!"

***Mary Howitt***

# NIGHT AND MICE

## MADAM MOUSE TROTS

### "Dame Souris trotte grise dans le noir" – Verlaine

Madam Mouse trots,
Grey in the black night!
Madam Mouse trots;
furred is the light.
The elephant-trunks
Trumpet from the sea ...
Grey in the black night
The mouse trots free.
Hoarse as a dog's bark
The heavy leaves are furled ...
The cat's in his cradle,
All's well with the world.

***Edith Sitwell***

# MOONLIT APPLES

At the top of the house the apples are laid in rows,
And the skylight lets the moonlight in, and those
Apples are deep-sea apples of green. There goes
A cloud on the moon in the autumn night.

A mouse in the wainscot scratches, and scratches, and then
There is no sound at the top of the house of men
Or mice; and the cloud is blown, and the moon again
Dapples the apples with deep-sea light.

They are lying in rows there, under the gloomy beams;
On the sagging floor; they gather the silver streams
Out of the moon, those moonlit apples of dreams,
And quiet is the steep stair under.

In the corridors under there is nothing but sleep.
And stiller than ever on orchard boughs they keep
Tryst with the moon, and deep is the silence, deep
On moon-washed apples of wonder.

***John Drinkwater***

# CATS AND MICE

## CATS AND MICE

Lets take a cat, and foster him well with milk,
And tender flesh, and make his couch of silk,
And let him see a mouse go by the wall;
Anon he waiveth milk, and flesh, and all,
And every dainty that is in the house,
Such appetite hath he to eat a mouse.

***Geoffrey Chaucer***

## MICE AND CAT

One mouse, two mice,
Three mice, four,
Stealing from their tunnel,
Creeping through the door.

Softly! softly!
Don't make a sound –
Don't let your little feet
Patter on the ground.

There on the hearthrug,
Sleek and fat,
Soundly sleeping,
Lies old Tom Cat.

If he should hear you,
There'd be no more
Of one mouse, two mice,
Three mice, four.

So please be careful
How far you roam,
For if you should wake him ...
He'd-chase-you-all-HOME!

***Clive Sansom***

# DEATH OF A CAT

Alas! Mowler, the children's pride,
Has slipped on a water-butt, tumbled inside
And died.

The seamstress on her sewing machine
Stitched a shroud of satin sheen.

The carpenter hammered and planed a coffin
Of seasoned oak without a knot in.

The sexton – he loved dear Mowler well –
Mournfully, mournfully tolled the bell.

Few were the prayers the parson spoke.
All he could do, poor fellow, was choke.

But saddest of all in the funeral train
Were the children. Deep were their sorrow and pain,

For they knew, as they followed the churchyard through,
They'd never set eyes on Mowler again.

In silence behind the coffin they stepped,
Solemnly, slowly. Everyone wept

Except
The little mice hid in the hedge – not they!
'Twas not *their* hearts that bled.
"Let's out and play,"
They cried. "Oh, spread
The butter thick on the bread!
Dance in cream cheese right up to our knees,
For the cat is dead!
Hooray!
The cat
is
dead!"

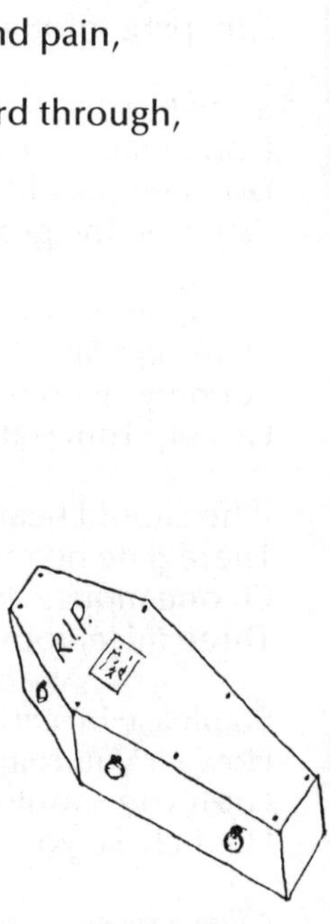


***Ian Serraillier***

# SIX LITTLE MICE

Six little mice sat down to spin.
Pussy passed by and she peeped in.
"What are you doing, my fine little men?"
"Weaving coats for gentlemen."
"Shall I come in and cut off your threads?"
"No, No, Mistress Pussy, you'd bite off our heads."
"Oh, no, I'll not; I'll help you to spin."
"That may be so, but you don't come in."

***Anon***

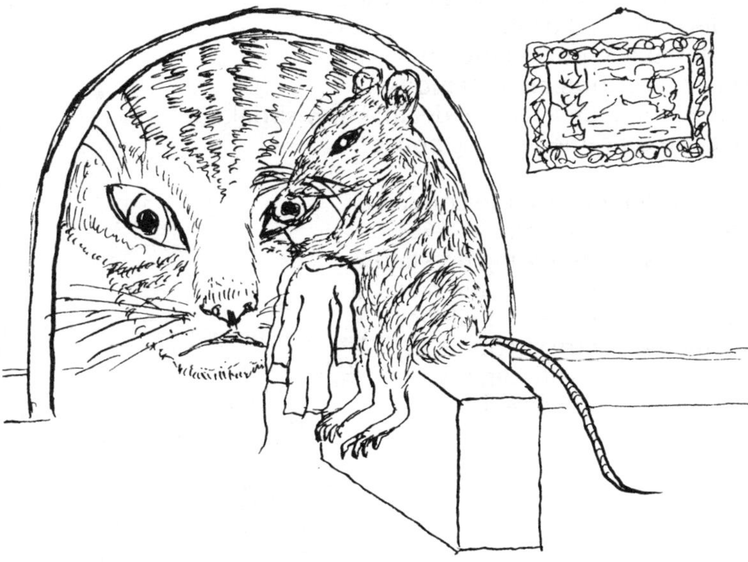

# CATCHING THE CAT

The mice had met in council,
They all looked haggard and worn,
For the state of affairs was too terrible
To be any longer borne.
Not a family out of mourning, –
There was crape on every hat, –
They were desperate – something must be done
And done at once, to the cat.

Then rather an old mouse rose, and said:
"It might prove a possible thing
To set the trap which they set for us –
That one with the awful spring!"
The suggestion was applauded
Loudly by one and all,
Till somebody squeaked: "That trap would be
About ninety-five times too small!"

Then a medical mouse suggested
(A little under his breath):
"If you confiscate the very first mouse
That dies a natural death,
I'll undertake to poison the cat,
If you'll let me prepare that mouse."
"There's not been a natural death," they shrieked,
"Since the cat came into the house!"

The smallest mouse in the council
Arose with a solemn air,
And, by way of increasing his stature,
Rubbed up his whiskers and hair.
He waited until there was silence
All along the pantry shelf,
And then he said with dignity,
"*I* will catch the cat myself!

"When next I hear her coming,
Instead of running away,
I shall turn and face her boldly,
And pretend to be at play.
She will not see her danger,
Poor creature! I suppose;
But as she stoops to catch me,
I shall catch her, by the nose!"

The mice began to look hopeful,
Yes, even the old ones, when
A grey-haired mouse said slowly,
"And what will you do with her then?"
The champion, disconcerted,
Replied with dignity, "Well –
I think, if you'll excuse me,
'Twould be wiser not to tell!

"We all have our inspirations," –
This produced a general smirk, –
"But we are not all at liberty
To explain just how they'll work.
I ask you simply to trust me;
You need have no further fears –
Consider our enemy done for!"
The council gave three cheers.

"I do believe she's coming!"
Said a small mouse nervously.
"Run if you like," said the champion,
"But I shall wait and see!"
And sure enough she was coming –
The mice all scampered away,
Except the noble champion,
Who had made up his mind to stay.

The mice had faith, – of course they had,
They were all of them trusting souls, –
But a sort of general feeling
Kept them safely in their holes,
Until some time in the evening;
Then the boldest ventured out,
And there he saw in the distance
The cat prance gaily about!

There was dreadful consternation,
Till some one at last said, "Oh,
He's not had time to do it,
Let us not prejudge him so!"
"I believe in him, of course I do,"
Said the nervous mouse with a sigh,
"But the cat looks uncommonly happy,
And I wish I *did* know why!"

That cat, I regret to mention,
Still prances about that house,
And no message, letter, or telegram
Has come from the champion mouse.
The mice are a little discouraged;
The demand for crape goes on;
They feel they'd be happier if they knew
Where the champion mouse has gone.

This story has a moral, –
It is very short you'll see, –
So, of course, you all will listen,
For fear of offending me.
It is well to be courageous,
And valiant, and all that,
But – if you are mice – you'd better think twice,
Before you catch the cat.

***Margaret Vandergrift Janvier***

# THE PRAYER OF THE MOUSE

I am so little and grey,
dear God,
how can You keep me in mind?
Always spied upon,
always chased.
Nobody ever gives me anything,
and I nibble meagrely at life.
Why do they reproach me with being a mouse?
Who made me but You?
I only ask to stay hidden.
Give me my hunger's pittance
safe from the claws
of that devil with green eyes.
Amen.

*Carmen Bernos de Gasztold*

# THOUGHTS OF A WELL-READ CAT
## On observing a tell-tale hole in the wainscot

To mouse, or not to mouse – that is the question,
Whether 'tis better in all conscience to suffer
The cheek and squeak of rodent merriment
Or to out claws against this sea of insolence
And by quick pawing, end them?

*Elizabeth Critchfield*

# TOWN AND COUNTRY

## CITY MOUSE AND GARDEN MOUSE

The city mouse lives in a house;
The garden mouse lives in a bower,
He's friendly with the frogs and toads,
And sees the pretty plants in flower.

The city mouse eats bread and cheese;
The garden mouse eats what he can;
We will not grudge him seeds and stocks,
Poor little timid furry man.

*Christina Rossetti*

## THE COUNTRY MOUSE AND THE CITY MOUSE

In a snug little cot lived a fat little mouse,
Who enjoyed, unmolested, the range of the house;
With plain food content, she would breakfast on cheese,
She dined upon bacon, and supped on grey peas.

A friend from the town to the cottage did stray,
And he said he was come a short visit to pay;
So the mouse spread her table as gay as you please,
And brought the nice bacon and charming grey peas.

The visitor frowned, and he thought to be witty:
Cried he, "You must know, I am come from the city,
Where we all should be shocked at provisions like these,
For we never eat bacon and horrid grey peas.

"To town come with me, I will give you a treat:
Some excellent food, most delightful to eat.
With me shall you feast just as long as you please;
Come, leave this fat bacon and shocking grey peas."

This kind invitation she could not refuse,
And the city mouse wished not a moment to lose;
Reluctant she quitted the fields and the trees,
The delicious fat bacon and charming grey peas.

They slily crept under a gay parlour door,
Where a feast had been given the evening before;
And it must be confessed they on dainties did sieze,
Far better than bacon, or even grey peas.

Here were custard and trifle, and cheesecakes good store,
Nice sweetmeats and jellies, and twenty things more;
All that art had invented the palate to please,
Except some fat bacon and smoking grey peas.

They were nicely regaling, when into the room
Came the dog and the cat, and the maid with a broom:
They jumped in a custard both up to their knees;
The country mouse sighed for her bacon and peas.

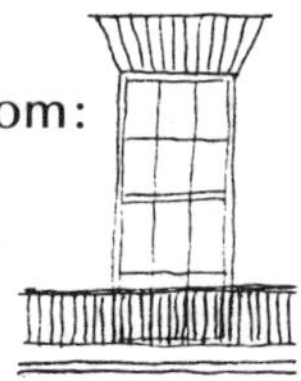

Cried she to her friend, "Get me safely away,
I can venture no longer in London to stay;
For if oft you receive interruptions like these,
Give me my nice bacon and charming grey peas.

"Your living is splendid and gay, to be sure,
But the dread of disturbance you ever endure;
*I* taste true delight in contentment and ease,
And I *feast* on fat bacon and charming grey peas."

***Richard Scrafton Sharpe***

# OF MICE AND GOD

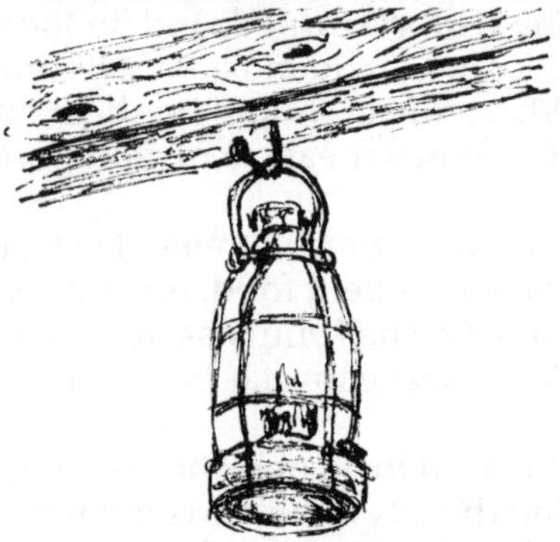

## THE SATIN MICE CREAKING LAST SUMMER'S GRASS

The satin mice creaking last summer's grass
Come on dry wine of miraculous clover;
They know; their eyes sprinkle the barn with stars;
They have no history to seal their sharp eyes over.
The pullets on the rafters in the henhouse,
Cockrels, whose eyes see through earth's crust
And track the midnight sun, believe tomorrow
Will strew incredible kernels in their dust.
Only the farmer fumbling, cold and slow,
With his pail and pitchfork does not know.

Every last white-eared sheep in the pen turns amber
At her trusting eyes in the lantern light,
Remembers, without memory, such another
Frosty time and wild wings snowing the night.
The cows know, without knowledge, it once happened,
And happen again in this new barn it may;
Their eyes grow large and tremulous foreseeing
The sun like a gentle daisy in their hay.
Even the milker stroking warm teats half believes
Such things as gods could be on Christmas Eves.

***Robert P. Tristram Coffin***

# MICE IN THE HAY

out of the lamplight
        *whispering worshipping*
the mice in the hay

timid eyes pearl-bright
        *whispering worshipping*
whisking quick and away

They were there that night
        *whispering worshipping*
smaller than snowflakes are

quietly made their way
        *whispering worshipping*
close to the manger

yes, they were afraid
        *whispering worshipping*
as the journey was made

from a dark corner
        *whispering worshipping*
scuttling together

But He smiled to see them
        *whispering worshipping*
there in the lamplight

stretched out His hand to them
they saw the baby King
hurried back out of sight
        *whispering worshipping*

***Leslie Norris***

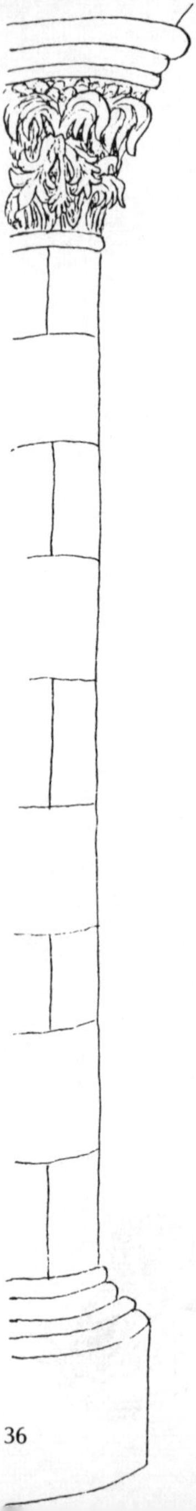

# DIARY OF A CHURCH MOUSE

Here among long-discarded cassocks,
Damp stools, and half-split open hassocks,
Here where the Vicar never looks
I nibble through old service books.
Lean and alone I spend my days
Behind this Church of England baize.
I share my dark forgotten room
With two oil-lamps and half a broom.
The cleaner never bothers me,
So here I eat my frugal tea.
My bread is sawdust mixed with straw;
My jam is polish for the floor.
        Christmas and Easter may be feasts
For congregations and for priests,
And so may Whitsun. All the same,
They do not fill my meagre frame.
For me the only feast at all
Is Autumn's Harvest Festival,
When I can satisfy my want
With ears of corn around the font.
I climb the eagle's brazen head
To burrow through a loaf of bread.
I scramble up the pulpit stair
And gnaw the marrows hanging there.
        It is enjoyable to taste
These items ere they go to waste,
But how annoying when one finds
That other mice with pagan minds
Come into church my food to share
Who have no proper business there.
Two field mice who have no desire
To be baptized, invade the choir.
A large and most unfriendly rat
Comes in to see what we are at.
He says he thinks there is no God
And yet he comes . . . it's rather odd.

This year he stole a sheaf of wheat
(It screened our special preacher's seat),
And prosperous mice from fields away
Come in to hear the organ play,
And under cover of its notes
Ate through the altar's sheaf of oats.
A Low Church mouse, who thinks that I
Am too papistical, and High,
Yet somehow doesn't think it wrong
To munch through Harvest Evensong,
While I, who starve the whole year through,
Must share my food with rodents who
Except at this time of the year
Not once inside the church appear.
        Within the human world I know
Such goings-on could not be so,
For human beings only do
What their religion tells them to.
They read the Bible every day
And always, night and morning, pray,
And just like me, the good church mouse,
Worship each week in God's own house.
        But all the same it's strange to me
How very full the church can be
With people I don't see at all
Except at Harvest Festival.

***John Betjeman***

# BROTHER MOUSE

There were feet first,
Close to the edge of the thicket
Of corn where I hid, cowering
At the side of the field
Where the green grass sloped away
And the sheep fed.
And then the world
Hung on a voice that was sunlight
And morning peace.
The little birds dropped
Out of the sky, and their singing
Stopped at his word,
Though not for long.
Bread fell from above like rain,
And all again was song.
And I, the mouse,
Thought suddenly, – "This is for me,"
And scurried out
Into the light
Where the sun was and the Brother Man.
His hand came down
Out of the blue
Ahead of his brown and laughing eyes
And rested there,
Close where I was,
Cupped. I climbed,
Answering my quick heart's longing,
And was lifted up
Into another world,
High above cornfield and my hidden home.
The other hand touched with finger
My brown fur.
And then he put me down
On earth again.
What next was I supposed to do?

Leave that warm fur of mother,
Down of nest,
Safe haven, –
A moment's promise,
Not for ever?
I scurried down
And ate a crumb
And bore another, not to forget
Back into the thicket
That was my own, known world,
But no longer all I knew.

***Steuart Allin***

# NUNC DIMITTIS

A little mouse died
And went to Heaven;
He climbed many stairs,
Seven thousand times seven.
Eventually arrived
At Heaven's Gate,
Rather puffed
And afraid he'd be late.
"You can't come in here,"
Frowned St Peter,
"You're scruffy and small,
We want something neater."
"Oh dear!" said the mouse,
As he stifled a sigh,
And with one tiny paw
Wiped a tear from his eye.
As he turned round to go,
Another voice roared;
St Peter, he trembled.
This voice was the Lord.
"And why can't this creature
Come into My House;
Are we so overcrowded
There's no room for a Mouse?
A Mouse, furthermore
Whose record's unblemished.
A sharer of food
(Though himself often famished);
A Mouse who cared
Not for self, but for others,
Who cherished his parents
His sisters, his brothers."
After a pause
The Lord carried on,
More quietly, now
His anger had gone.

"See here, Peter,
Let's get this straight.
I decide who comes
Through the Gate.
Not you, or the angels,
Wise though you are.
Not even Il Papa
Or Cantuar."
St Peter stood back,
Concealing his chagrin;
Opened the gates
And the Mouse scampered in,
Wide-eyed in wonder
As he gazed round God's House.
God smiled on St Peter
And winked at the Mouse.

***Elizabeth Critchfield***

# DAY OF THESE DAYS

Such a morning it is when love
leans through geranium windows
and calls with a cockerel's tongue.

When red-haired girls scamper like roses
over the rain-green grass,
and the sun drips honey.

When hedgerows grow venerable,
berries dry black as blood,
and holes suck in their bees.

Such a morning it is when mice
run whispering from the church,
dragging dropped ears of harvest.

When the partridge draws back his spring
and shoots like a buzzing arrow
over grained and mahogany fields.

When no table is bare,
and no breast dry,
and the tramp feeds off ribs of rabbit.

Such a day it is when time
piles up the hills like pumpkins,
and the streams run golden.

When all men smell good,
and the cheeks of girls
are as baked bread to the mouth.

As bread and beanflowers
the touch of their lips,
and their white teeth sweeter than cucumbers.

***Laurie Lee***

# OF MICE AND MEN

## SMALL PREFERENCE

While most people are agreed that cats
Are infinitely preferable to rats,
I think mice are
Nicer.

***Iain Kendell***

## CALL UP BEATRIX POTTER

That nutbrown fieldmouse
Nibbling my bulbs will never
Earn me royalties.

***Harold Morland***

# THE MEADOW MOUSE

In a shoebox stuffed in an old nylon stocking
Sleeps the baby mouse I found in the meadow,
Where he trembled and shook beneath a stick
Till I caught him up by the tail and brought him in,
Cradled in my hand,
A little quaker, the whole body of him trembling,
His absurd whiskers sticking out like a cartoon-mouse,
His feet like small leaves,
Little lizard-feet,
Whitish and spread wide when he tried to struggle away,
Wriggling like a miniscule puppy.

Now he's eaten his three kinds of cheese and drunk from
        his bottle-cap watering-trough –
So much he just lies in one corner,
His tail curled under him, his belly big
As his head; his bat-like ears
Twitching, tilting towards the least sound.

Do I imagine he no longer trembles
When I come close to him?
He seems no longer to tremble.

But this morning the shoe-box on the back porch is empty.
Where has he gone, my meadow mouse,
My thumb of a child that nuzzled in my palm? –
To run under the hawk's wing,
Under the eye of the great owl watching from the elm-tree,
To live by courtesy of the shrike, the snake, the tom-cat.

I think of the nestling fallen into the deep grass,
The turtle gasping in the dusty rubble of the highway,
The paralytic stunned in the tub, and the water rising, –
All things innocent, hapless, forsaken.

***Theodore Roethke***

# MOUSE

I cursed the mouse that gnawed my cheese
And trespassed smoothly on my peace.

I growled and vowed I'd do him in –
The wretched scrap of speed and sin!

"You haunt my dreams and days," I cried;
"For my bread's sake it's time you died!"

I laughed to find my cunning trap
Had killed the beastly little chap.

The little chap! Yes, that's the name
I used in death and stood in shame.

The story of that righteous deed
Is now a sword on which I bleed.

***Clifford Dyment***

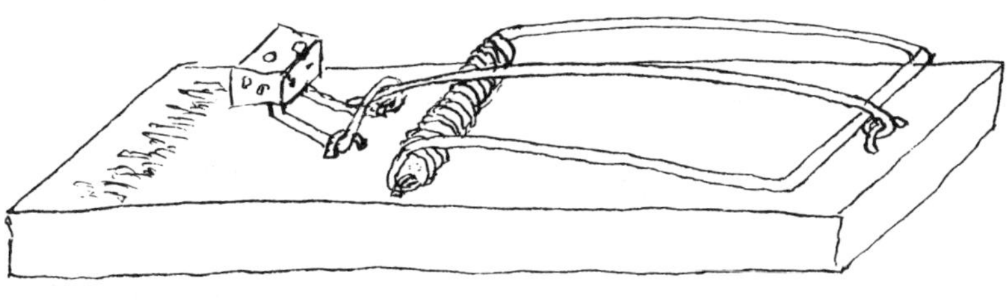

# MOUSE IN THE HOUSE

## THE LITTLE MOUSE

I have seen you, little mouse,
Running all about our house,
Through the hole your little eye
In the wainscot peeping sly,
Hoping soon some crumbs to steal,
To make quite a hearty meal.
Look before you venture out,
See if pussy is about;
If she's gone you'll quickly run
To the larder for some fun;
Round about the dishes creep;
Taking into each a peep,
To choose the daintiest that's there,
Spoiling things you do not care.

***Anon***

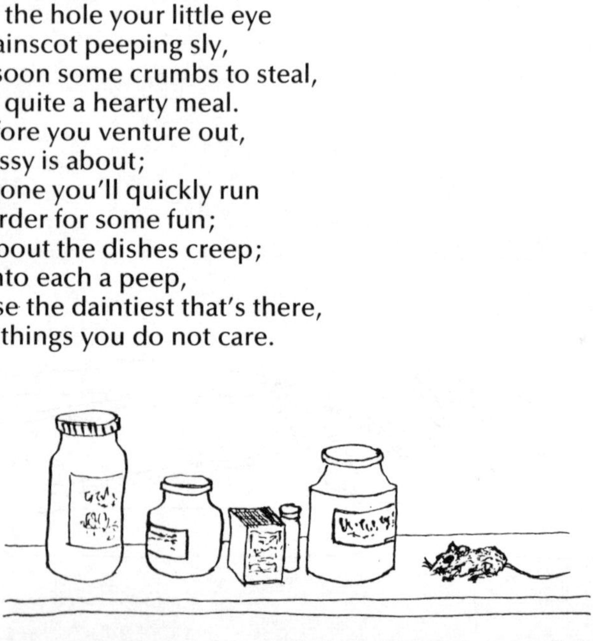

# THE MOUSE

I hear a mouse
Bitterly complaining
In a crack of moonlight
Aslant on the floor –

"Little I ask
And that little is not granted.
There are few crumbs
In this world any more.

"The breadbox is tin
And I cannot get in.

"The jam's in a jar
My teeth cannot mar.

"The cheese sits by itself
On the pantry shelf.

"All night I run
Searching and seeking,
All night I run
About on the floor.

"Moonlight is there
And a bare place for dancing,
But no little feast
Is spread any more."

***Elizabeth Coatsworth***

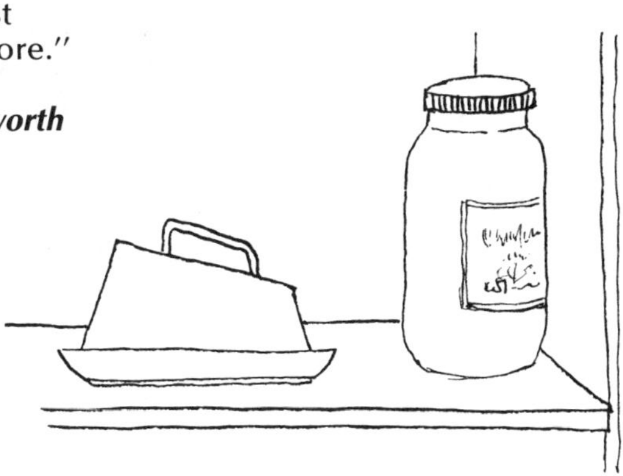

## INVITATION TO A MOUSE

There's pudding in the pantry,
        There's jam upon the shelf,
There's bacon in a pastry-pie
        On a dish of delf –
Mousiekin, wee Mousiekin,
        Go and help yourself!
But please, Mousie, Please,
Don't touch the toasted cheese,
For if you do mayhap
Something will go snap!
And the pudding and the jam
And the pastry and the ham
Will have to stay untasted, all wasted
        on the shelf.

***Eleanor Farjeon***

## MOUSE

Brown Mouse;
Whisker wiffling
Cheese eating
Mouse.

Shy Mouse;
Cupboard creeping
Nut nibbling
Mouse.

Friendly Mouse;
Night rustling
Silence breaking
House mouse.

***Elizabeth Critchfield***

Me up at does

out of the floor
quietly Stare

a poisoned mouse

still alive

is asking What
have i done that

You wouldn't have

***e e cummings***

# THE MOUSE'S PETITION

## Found in the trap, where he had been confined all night

O hear a pensive prisoner's prayer,
For liberty that sighs;
And never let thine heart be shut
Against the wretch's cries!

For here forlorn and sad I sit
Within the wiry grate;
And tremble at the approaching morn,
Which brings impending fate.

If e'er thy breast with freedom glowed
And spurned a tyrant's chain,
Let not thy strong oppressive force
A free-born mouse detain.

O do not stain with guiltless blood
Thy hospitable hearth;
Nor triumph that thy wiles betrayed
A prize so little worth!

The scattered gleanings of a feast
My frugal meals supply:
But if thine unrelenting heart
That slender boon deny,

The cheerful light, the vital air,
Are blessings widely given;
Let nature's commoners enjoy
The common gifts of heaven.

The well-taught philosophic mind
To all compassion gives,
Casts round the world an equal eye,
And feels for all that lives.

***Anna Laetitia Barbauld***

# THE MOUSE

I live in sober Suffolk
In a dim and sober house,
And I share this dim sobriety
With a noble, sober mouse.

On an eager April morning
I discovered that the mouse
Had minced a First Edition
To lend comfort to its house.

I set a trap to catch the mouse,
I baited it with cheese,
And bacon-rind, and honeycomb,
The harvest of my bees.

The mouse was caught, it looked at me
With eyes of velvet brown,
It looked at me, I looked at it.
I could not set it down.

Of course I should have drowned it,
It was weak of me, but oh,
The velvet eyes were starred with hope –
I had to let it go.

But all who gaze in velvet eyes
Must pay the settled price,
And now my First Edition warms
Some newly publish'd mice.

***Walter Meade***

# MOUSE

A small mouse
comes every night
to clean my house
by moonlight.

When in my bed
I sleep sound,
like someone dead,
it glides around

the four walls,
the earthen floor.
No crumb falls
unaccounted for.

Starlight or storm,
it matters not:
the dawn's alarm,
the creaking cot

trouble it less
than that I may
rudely miss
supper one day.

My floor is clean,
my table clear:
my mouse has been
gleaning here.

It cannot be
so very fat.
My poverty
must see to that –

but then I know
it cannot be lean:
my house is so
uncommon clean!

***Kenneth MacKenzie***

# THE MERRY MICE

The merry mice stay in their holes,
And hide there all the day;
But when the house is still at night,
The rogues come out and play!

They climb upon the pantry shelf,
And taste of all they please;
They drink the milk that's set for cream,
And nibble bread and cheese.

But if they chance to hear the cat,
Their feast will soon be done;
They scamper off to hide themselves
As fast as they can run.

***Anon.***

# PETS

## TAKE ONE HOME FOR THE KIDDIES

On shallow straw, in shadeless glass,
Huddled by empty bowls, they sleep:
No dark, no dam, no earth, no grass –
*Mam, get us one of them to keep.*

Living toys are something novel,
But it soon wears off somehow.
Fetch the shoebox, fetch the shovel –
*Mam, we're playing funerals now.*

***Philip Larkin***

# THE MICE

Brian Fleming sniffed the mice
And let them fur through his fingers,
Drove them through the wheel device
Scratching claw,
Pink-twitching up the ladder
To the bedroom where the straw,
Spongy-with-mouse-smell
Bedding starts to breathe and swell.

Brian Fleming watched them climb,
Scrabbling at the no-wall barrier,
Twitched his nose in window-mime,
Felt through the glass their baffled scratching;
Lifted high,
Pink-pinched and legs jerking,
A soft body, suddenly shy
Of his own tenderness. The thought ran,
"This box is like our caravan".

He kept the pets with fierce pride
And scowled away the playtime lout,
The boldest dared not take a stick
To drive the sun-warmed sleepers out.

They called him "muzzard" but kept clear,
And sneered at him for teacher's pet;
He raged at this and teachers sighed
At the least biddable they'd met.

Late in one day for some misdeed
He found a mocking, yelling horde,
Heard cries of, "Dare yer; cruel; scared,"
And crept beneath the easel board.

And watched, and caught, "Clive's got a match."
"I dare yer set the straw alight."
And when he pounced with clawing hands
The boys leapt back with gapes of fright.

He punched and thumped and shoved his way
And got his fingers in Clive's hair,
And banged Clive's head against the sink,
And bruised Clive's back against a chair.

They pulled him off and Fleming stood
Trembling with anger, nostrils white,
And to the teacher's questions said,
"He tried to set my mice alight."

And when they'd wiped away the blood,
And stitched Clive's head and sent him home,
They questioned Brian for an hour
And shrank him to a tired gnome.

"Come to no good," the teachers said;
The Head was puzzled, "Didn't know";
The child psychologist was called,
And jerked his head and stood tip-toe,

Rocked to his heels, and turned his gaze
On Brian standing in the dock,
And thumbed his glasses round his ears,
And mumbled about traumatic shock.

And Brian watched with lowered eyes,
And heard the words about him weave;
He twisted fingers, scratched his leg,
And wiped his nose upon his sleeve.

But he had stopped their little game
With matches and the lighted straw;
He could still feel his sudden strength
Banging Clive's head upon the floor;

Banging his head against a wheel –
For Carters' van had set on fire,
And screams inside were choked and quenched
While bannered flame waved round the pyre.

For Brian Fleming then had seen
The neighbours scramble acorn-buckets,
The bonfire where the van had been,
The scaly charcoal of a wheel,
A doll forgotten in wet grass,
The next-door van beginning to peel;
No hessian screen could try to hide
What charred and shrivelled him inside.

***Gregory Harrison***

# THE LAMENT OF THE WHITE MOUSE

We shared in one delightful house;
    We shared a mossy bed.
I never knew another mouse
    Than her – and she is dead.

The beady eye, the nimble strength,
    The soft and silken fur!
The whiskers, and the noble length
    Of tail that followed her!

And now I'm lonely in the run,
    And lonely on the stair,
And lonely in the nest we spun –
    So warm when she was there!

The wheel she loved to turn is still.
    The feet that ran so light
Have twinkled up the heavenly hill
    And tread the wheel of night.

***E.V. Rieu***

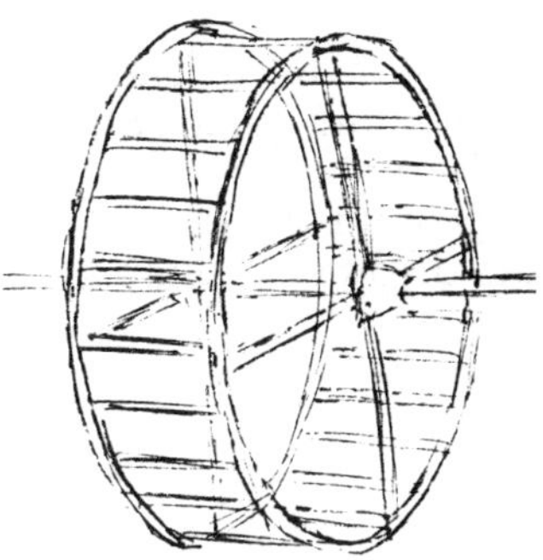

# MOUSE STORIES

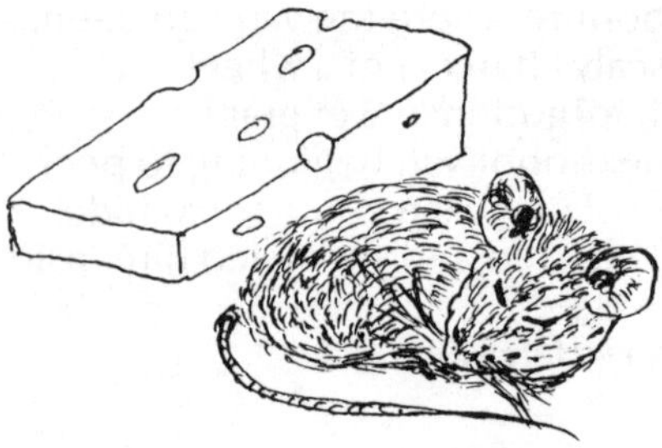

## THREE MICE

Three little mice walked into town,
Their coats were grey, and their eyes were brown.

Three little mice went down the street,
With woolwork slippers upon their feet.

Three little mice sat down to dine
On curranty bread and gooseberry wine.

Three little mice ate on and on,
Till every crumb of the bread was gone.

Three little mice, when the feast was done,
Crept home quietly one by one.

Three little mice went straight to bed,
And dreamt of crumbly, curranty bread.

***Charlotte Druitt Cole***

# THE MOUSE AND THE FIRE ENGINES

Here is a house, a neat little place
With antimacassars and curtains of lace,
That stood in a street in Stirling.

Here is a mouse
That appeared in the house,
A neat little place,
With curtains of lace
That stood in a street in Stirling.

Here is Miss Simpson who uttered a yell
As out of the house she rushed pell-mell
At the sight of the mouse
That appeared in her house,
A neat little place
With curtains of lace
That stood in a street in Stirling.

Here is a boy who sings in the choir
Running and waving and shouting "Fire!"
When little Miss Simpson uttered a yell
As out of the house she rushed pell-mell
At the sight of the mouse
That appeared in her house,
A neat little place
With curtains of lace
That stood in a street in Stirling.

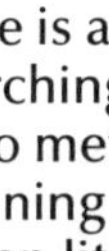

Here is a policeman on his beat
Marching with dignity down the street,
Who met the boy who sings in the choir,
Running and waving and shouting "Fire!"
When little Miss Simpson uttered a yell
As out of the house she rushed pell-mell
At the sight of the mouse
That appeared in her house,
A neat little place
With curtains of lace
That stood in a street in Stirling.

Here is the operator clearing the line
For somebody dialling 999;
For the dignified policeman went from his beat
To the telephone box at the end of the street
When he met the boy who sings in the choir,
Running and waving and shouting "Fire!"
When little Miss Simpson uttered a yell
As out of the house she rushed pell-mell
At the sight of the mouse
That appeared in her house,
A neat little place
With curtains of lace
That stood in a street in Stirling.

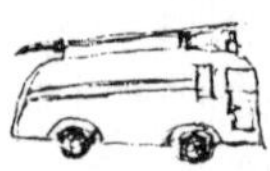

Here are the fire engines, three or four,
Their bells are ringing, their engines roar;
For the telephone girl has cleared the line
For somebody dialling 999;
For the dignified policeman went from his beat
To the telephone box at the end of the street
When he met the boy who sings in the choir,
Running and waving and shouting "Fire!"
When little Miss Simpson uttered a yell
As out of the house she rushed pell-mell
At the sight of the mouse
That appeared in her house,
A neat little place
With curtains of lace
That stood in a street in Stirling.

Here is Miss Simpson who, much upset,
Has a narrow escape from getting wet;
For the firemen propose
To turn on the hose,
Without pause to inquire
Whereabouts is the fire,
But Miss Simpson calls out at the very last minute
That this is *her* house and there's not a fire in it.
It's a neat little place
With curtains of lace
That stood in a street in Stirling.

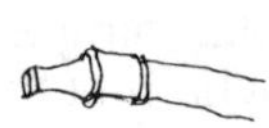

Here are the firemen coiling their hose.
They jump on the engines and everyone goes,
Bicycles, cars and folk on their feet,
Even the policeman returns to his beat,
Then the boy and Miss Simpson search for the mouse,
From attic to cellar they ransack the house,
A neat little place,
With curtains of lace
That stood in a street in Stirling.

Here is the magistrate frowning next day
And stating severely that someone must pay
For fire engines' petrol and firemen's wages,
And ferreting out by steps and stages
What is the name
Of the person to blame,
Wishful to find and to punish the same.
The policeman declared that he couldn't decline
To dial the number 999.
The choirboy explained how he made the mistake,
And little Miss Simpson, all of a quake,
Told of the mouse
That appeared in her house,
A neat little place
With curtains of lace
That stood in a street in Stirling.

At length the Magistrate cleared his throat,
And first he said and then he wrote:
"The fire engines it seems were summoned in error,
Due to Miss Simpson's screams of terror;
So the mouse that caused them must bear the blame.
But, since no one can find and punish the same,
Stirling Town Council must pay the cost
And, doubtless, recover the money so lost
By raising the rates on each neat little place,
With antimacassars and curtains of lace,
That stands in the streets of Stirling."

***Wilma Horsburgh***

# THE MOUSE AND THE CAKE

A mouse found a beautiful piece of plum cake,
The richest and sweetest that mortal could make;
'Twas heavy with citron and fragrant with spice,
And covered with sugar all sparkling as ice.

"My stars!" cried the mouse, while his eye beamed with glee,
"Here's a treasure I've found: what a feast it will be;
But, hark! there's a noise, 'tis my brothers at play;
So I'll hide with the cake, lest they wander this way.

"Not a bit shall they have, for I know I can eat
Every morsel myself, and I'll have such a treat."
So off went the mouse as he held the cake fast;
While his hungry young brothers went scampering past.

He nibbled, and nibbled, and panted, but still
He kept gulping it down till he made himself ill;
Yet he swallowed it all, and 'tis easy to guess,
He was soon so unwell that he groaned with distress.

His family heard him, and as he grew worse,
They sent for the doctor, who made him rehearse
How he'd eaten the cake to the very last crumb,
Without giving his playmates and relatives some.

"Ah me!" cried the doctor, "advice is too late;
You must die before long, so prepare for your fate;
If you had but divided the cake with your brothers,
'Twould have done you no harm, and been good for the others.

"Had you shared it, the treat had been wholesome enough;
But eaten by *one,* it was dangerous stuff;
So prepare for the worst -" and the word had scarce fled,
When the doctor turned round, and the patient was dead.

Now all little people the lesson may take,
And *some* large ones may learn from the mouse and the cake;
Not to be over-selfish with what we may gain,
Or the best of our pleasures may turn into pain.

***Eliza Cook***

# TAILPIECE

The little mouse doth skip and play
He runs by night and sleeps by day.

***Anon***

**For further information and news of forthcoming
Triple Cat paperbacks send for a brochure to:
TRIPLE CAT PUBLISHING
3 Back Lane Cottages, Bucks Horn Oak, Farnham, Surrey GU10 4LN**